Tantalizing Turkey: 60 #Delish Recipes for Turkeys & Leftovers

RHONDA BELLE

Copyright © 2016 Rhonda Belle

All rights reserved.

ISBN-13: 978-1541176058

ISBN-10: 1541176057

DEDICATION

To Foodies Everywhere...Enjoy & Be Well!

Table of Contents

That Big Beautiful Bird…	1
Whole Turkeys	2
Creole-Stuffed Turkey	2
Deep Fried Turkey	2
Easy Orange Turkey	3
Fall Harvest Glazed Turkey	3
Grecian Turkey with Pine Nuts	4
Grilled Whole Turkey	5
Heavenly Herbed Bird	5
Newlywed's First Stuffed Turkey	5
Rosemary Roasted Turkey	6
Savory Guatemalan Roast Turkey	7
Leftover & Select Turkey Cuts	8
Apple Turkey	8
Awesome Turkey Spinach Casserole (low fat)	8
Baked Turkey Mac N' Cheese	9
Celestial Citrus Turkey	9
Cheesy Tukey Omelets	9
Creamy Turkey Tortellini Alfredo	10
Curried Turkey	10
Delish Broccoli Salad	11
Drunken Turkey Dish	11
Easy Italian Turkey Salad	12
Fun Florentine Turkey Breast	13
Glorious Grape Turkey Salad	13
Green Bean Turkey Surprise	14
Hot Pepper Turkey Spread	15
Hot Turkey Salad	15
Island Dream Turkey Salad	16
Italian Turkey Pasta	16
Jamaican Turkey Sandwiches & Coleslaw	17
Lemon Turkey with Couscous Stuffing	17
Melon Medley Turkey Salad	18
Mucho Turkey Burrito	19
Navaho Turkey Soup	19
New Year's Turkey Salad	20
Pumpkin Turkey Chili	20
Roasted Turkey Walkers	21
Simple Turkey Mex	21
Slow Cooker Turkey Stew	22

Spicy Turkey Wraps with Strawberry Salsa	22
Stuffed Teriyaki Turkey Legs	23
Sunny Turkey Salad	23
Terrific Turkey Enchiladas	23
Top-Notch Turkey Casserole	24
Sumptuous Turkey & Mushrooms	25
Turkey Citrus Salad	26
Turkey Pasta Divine	26
Turkey Stuffed Peppers	27
Turkey Tetrazzini Delight	28
Turkey Wild Rice Soup	29
White Turkey Chili	29
Easy & Elegant Turkey Stuffing	31
World's Best Turkey Gravy	31

That Big Beautiful Bird...

When it comes to the holiday season, turkey is often the main attraction of family gatherings and meals. The large birds can be prepared in several traditional ways and many unique ones, including roasted, baked, slow cooked, grilled, and fried. Leftovers are just as tasty because many of the seasonings and flavors have had time to set. With a little ingenuity, turkey leftovers can turn one meal into many.

A few helpful tips will keep your turkey enjoyment festive and safe...

- Keep work surfaces (and hands) clean and sanitized. Uncooked poultry can contaminate things easily. Keep raw meat away from other foods.
- Always defrost frozen turkeys, but not on the countertop. Defrost the bird (one day of thawing for every four pounds of turkey). Be sure to thaw turkey in the fridge or a sink of cold water that is refreshed every half hour. If turkey is exposed to room temperature for over two hours or more, it can quickly become unsafe. Know that anything between 40°F and 140°F is of concern and bacteria can grow rapidly.
- You can cook stuffing in an oven safe casserole dish separately if desired, which can help ensure thorough cooking. If you prefer to stuff your bird, only do so just before sliding it in the oven or other chosen method of preparation. The internal temp of the turkey should be at least 165°F.
- Turkey cooking times vary depending on the bird's overall weight. Up to four hours is common. Refer to labeling instructions for your bird.
- Roasting pans should have a bit of depth for proper basting which prevents a dry turkey. Anything 2" to 2.5" deep works well. You can also use foil to seal in moisture.
- Oven temps should be a minimum of 325°F. Roast turkey until a meat thermometer inserted into the thigh of the turkey reads an internal temperature as180°F and a thermometer inserted into the breast reads 165°-170°F.
- The turkey (with stuffing) should be allowed to stand for at least 20 minutes before carving. Also, within two hours after cooking, stuffing and most meat should be removed from bones and refrigerated.
- Leftover turkey meat is excellent in soups, salads, sandwiches, and other dishes like those included in this recipe collection. Holiday meal leftovers should be kept for only a limited period, generally 1-3 days max. This applies to stuffing, turkey, ham, pie, most veggies, and cranberry sauce. A month or two may be feasible if items are frozen.

Enjoy these great recipes and happy holidays to you and yours!

Whole Turkeys

Creole-Stuffed Turkey
¼ cup chopped celery
½ cup egg substitute
½ cup finely diced green pepper
½ cup finely diced sweet red pepper
¾ cup chopped smoked kielbasa
1 (8 pound) turkey
1 cup chicken broth
1 cup chopped fully cooked ham
2 ½ teaspoons Creole seasoning
2 cups cubed crustless day-old whole wheat bread
3 tablespoons finely diced onion
4 cups cubed corn bread
In a large bowl, combine all ingredients, saving broth for last to moisten. Just before baking, stuff the turkey. Skewer openings; tie drumsticks together. Place on a rack in a roasting pan. Bake at 325 degrees for up to 4 hours or until a meat thermometer reads 180 degrees for the turkey and 165 degrees for the stuffing. When the turkey begins to brown, cover lightly with aluminum foil and baste if needed. Remove all stuffing, carve and serve. #Delish!

Deep Fried Turkey
¼ cup Creole seasoning
1 (12 pound) whole turkey, neck and giblets removed
1 white onion
3 gallons peanut oil for frying, or as needed
In a large stockpot or turkey fryer, heat oil to 400 degrees. *Leave plenty of room to add turkey and prevent spill over.* Rinse turkey, and thoroughly pat dry with paper towels. Rub Creole seasoning over turkey inside and out. The neck hold should be open at least 2" for the free flow of oil. Next, place the whole onion and turkey in drain basket neck first. Slowly lower basket into hot oil to completely cover turkey. Maintain the temperature of the oil at 350 degrees, and cook turkey for 3 ½ minutes per pound, about 45 minutes. Carefully remove basket from oil, and drain the turkey. Insert a meat thermometer into the thickest part of the thigh until the internal temperature of the thigh reaches 180 degrees F (85 degrees C). Finish draining turkey on a paper layered with heat safe platter covered in newspaper or paper towels. Let rest for 10-15 minutes before carving. #Delish!

Easy Orange Turkey

½ (12 fluid ounce) can frozen orange juice concentrate, thawed
1 (16 pound) turkey
1 cup dry white wine
1 tablespoon black pepper
1 tablespoon dried oregano
1 tablespoon ground cumin
2 cups fresh lemon juice
2 tablespoons salt (or to taste)
3 heads garlic, peeled

Crush the peeled garlic cloves, and place into a large bowl. Season with pepper, cumin, oregano, and salt. Pour in lemon juice, wine, and orange juice concentrate. Whisk well. Using a sharp knife, pierce the turkey breast, thighs, and legs to allow the marinade to penetrate the meat. Pour the marinade over turkey, allowing it to flow into the holes, and follow by stuffing stuff garlic pieces into the holes. Cover the turkey well, and refrigerate overnight to marinate. Preheat oven to 325 degrees. Roast turkey until the internal temperature of the thickest part of the thigh measures 180 degrees F (80 degrees C), about 5 hours. Baste the turkey every 30 to 45 minutes. *Tip: When the breast has browned, cover bird loosely with aluminum foil to prevent burning.* Serve when done and enjoy!

Fall Harvest Glazed Turkey

¼ cup all-purpose flour
½ cup apple brandy
¾ cup butter, softened
1 (12 pound) whole turkey, neck and giblets reserved
1 ½ cups chopped carrots
1 ½ cups chopped celery
1 ½ teaspoons grated lemon zest
1 bay leaf
1/3 cup real maple syrup
2 ½ tablespoons chopped fresh thyme
2 cups apple cider
2 cups chopped onion
2 tablespoons chopped fresh marjoram
3 cups chicken broth
Salt and pepper to taste

Combine apple cider and maple syrup in a saucepan, and bring to a boil over medium-high heat. Continue cooking until reduced to ½ cup, then remove pan from heat. Stir in 1 tablespoon thyme, 1 tablespoon marjoram, and lemon zest. Stir in butter until melted, and season with salt and pepper. Cover, and refrigerate until cold. Preheat oven to 375 degrees. Place rack in lower third of oven. Place turkey on a rack set in a roasting pan. Reserve ¼ cup butter for gravy, and rub the remaining butter under the skin of the breast and over the outside of turkey. Arrange onion, celery, carrots turkey neck and giblets around the turkey. Sprinkle 1 tablespoon thyme and 1 tablespoon marjoram over vegetables. Pour 2 cups broth into pan. Next, place turkey in oven and roast for 30 minutes before reducing the oven temperature to 350 degrees. Cover entire turkey loosely with foil.

Continue roasting for about 2 ½ hours, or until the internal temperature of the thigh reaches 180 degrees F (85 degrees C). Transfer turkey to platter, and let stand 30 minutes. Strain the pan juices into a large measuring cup, and then remove any excess fat. Add enough chicken broth to pan juices to measure 3 cups. Transfer liquid to a saucepan, and bring to boil. In a small bowl, mix ¼ cup butter and 1/3 cup flour until smooth. Whisk flour and butter mixture into broth mixture. Stir in remaining thyme and the bay leaf. Boil until reduced to sauce consistency, stirring occasionally, about 10 minutes. Add apple brandy if desired. Season with salt and pepper to taste and enjoy. #Delish!

Grecian Turkey with Pine Nuts
¼ cup chopped onion
¼ cup orange juice
¼ cup pine nuts
¼ cup raisins (optional)
¼ cup tangerine juice
½ cup chicken broth
½ cup uncooked instant rice
½ pound ground beef
½ pound ground pork
½ teaspoon ground black pepper
1 (10 pound) whole turkey
1 cup chestnuts
1 teaspoon salt
1/3 cup butter
2 tablespoons brandy
2/3 cup butter
2/3 cup lemon juice
Salt and pepper to taste

Preheat oven to 325 degrees. Make a small incision on sides of each chestnut, and place in a skillet over medium heat. Cook, stirring often, until toasted. Remove from heat, peel, and chop. Next, melt 2/3 cup butter in a saucepan, and mix in the orange juice, tangerine juice, and lemon juice. Rub the turkey inside and out with the mixture, reserving some for basting. Season turkey with salt and pepper as desired. In a large skillet over medium heat, cook the ground beef, ground pork, and onion until beef and pork are evenly brown and onion is tender. Drain grease. Mix browned meat in the rice. Stir in the chestnuts, pine nuts, raisins, 1/3 cup butter, broth, and brandy. Season with 1 teaspoon salt and ½ teaspoon pepper. Continue cooking until all liquid has been absorbed. Next, stuff all turkey cavities with the mixture, and tie in place with kitchen twine. Place turkey on a rack in a roasting pan, and loosely cover breast and thighs with aluminum foil. Pour about ¼" water into the bottom of the pan. Maintain this level of water throughout cook time, adding more as needed. Roast turkey in the preheated oven for 3 to 4 hours, brushing occasionally with remaining butter and juice mixture. Increase oven temperature to 400 degrees during the final hour of roasting, and remove foil. Cook turkey until the internal temperature of the thigh reaches 180 degrees F (85 degrees C). Remove from oven, carve and serve. #Delish!

Grilled Whole Turkey
½ teaspoon chopped parsley
1 teaspoon paprika
1 teaspoon poultry seasoning
12 pounds whole turkey
2 cups water
2 teaspoons garlic powder
2 teaspoons onion powder
3 tablespoons chicken bouillon powder
Prepare an outdoor grill for medium heat. The heat should be indirect so as not to char the bird. Lightly oil grates. Rinse the turkey, and pat dry. Place turkey breast side down on the prepared grill. Sear turkey on both sides until skin is golden to dark brown. In a large roasting pan, mix together the water, bouillon powder, garlic powder, onion powder, poultry seasoning, parsley, and paprika. Place turkey breast side down in the roasting pan. Scoop the pan mixture over the turkey. Cover tightly with foil and place on grill. Grill 3 to 4 hours. Remove turkey from grill and let stand 15 minutes before carving. #Delish!

Heavenly Herbed Bird
½ teaspoon black pepper
¾ cup olive oil
1 teaspoon ground sage
1 teaspoon salt
1 (12 pound) whole turkey
2 cups water
2 teaspoons dried basil
2 tablespoons garlic powder
Preheat oven to 325 degrees. Clean turkey (discard giblets and organs), and place in a roasting pan with a lid. In a small bowl, combine olive oil, garlic powder, dried basil, ground sage, salt, and black pepper. Using a basting brush, apply the mixture to the outside of the uncooked turkey. Pour water into the bottom of the roasting pan, and cover. Bake for 3 to 3.5 hours, or until the internal temperature of the thigh reaches 180 degrees F (85 degrees C). Remove from oven and let stand 30 minutes before carving. #Delish!

Newlywed's First Stuffed Turkey
¼ cup chopped onion
1 (6 ounce) package dry bread stuffing mix
1 cup chopped celery
1 cup water
1 tablespoon butter
12 pounds whole turkey
2 tablespoons vegetable oil
4 slices toasted white bread, torn into small pieces
Salt and pepper to taste
Preheat oven to 350 degrees. Rinse turkey, remove giblets and place in a shallow roasting pan. Prepare stuffing per package directions. Melt butter

in a medium saucepan over medium heat, and slowly cook and stir celery and onion until tender. Mix celery, onion, and toasted bread pieces into the stuffing, and season with salt and pepper to taste. Next, scoop stuffing into the turkey body and neck cavity loosely. Rub the exterior of the turkey with vegetable oil and sprinkle with additional salt and pepper if desired. Loosely cover turkey with aluminum foil, and roast up to 4 hours in the preheated oven, until the thickest part of the thigh reaches 180 degrees F (85 degrees C) and the interior of the stuffing reaches 165 degrees F (70 degrees C). Remove foil during the last half hour of cooking to brown the bird. Remove from oven and let rest until dinner. #Delish!

Orange Glazed Turkey
¼ cup butter
1 (16 pound) whole turkey, neck and giblets removed
1 ½ teaspoons honey
1 orange, peeled, sectioned, and cut into bite-size pieces
1 pinch dried thyme
1/3 cup orange juice
1/3 cup orange marmalade
2 teaspoons rubbed sage
2 teaspoons salt

Preheat an oven to 325 degrees. Combine sage, salt, and thyme in a small bowl. Rub half of the sage mixture all over the turkey and place the turkey in a large roasting pan. Set remaining sage mixture aside. Next, bring butter, orange juice, orange marmalade, honey, and orange sections to a boil in a saucepan over medium-high heat. Reduce heat and simmer uncovered until thickened, stirring occasionally, 15 to 20 minutes. Stir in the remaining sage mixture. Brush the turkey with the glaze. Bake in the preheated oven for 5 hours and 30 minutes, basting every 30 minutes. Cover turkey lightly with foil and continue baking until no longer pink at the bone and the juices run clear, 30 minutes to 1 hour. Apply glaze liberally and often. An instant-read thermometer inserted into the thickest part of the thigh (near the bone) should read 180 degrees F (85 degrees C). Remove the turkey from the oven, cover with foil, and allow to rest for 10 to 15 minutes before serving. #Delish!

Rosemary Roasted Turkey
¾ cup olive oil
1 (12 pound) whole turkey
1 tablespoon chopped fresh basil
1 tablespoon Italian seasoning
1 teaspoon ground black pepper
Salt to taste
2 tablespoons chopped fresh rosemary
3 tablespoons minced garlic

Preheat oven to 325 degrees. In a small bowl, mix the olive oil, garlic, rosemary, basil, Italian seasoning, black pepper and salt. Set aside. Next, wash turkey inside and out; pat dry. Remove any large fat deposits and loosen the area between the breast meat and skin by slowly working your fingers between the two areas. Do this to the end of the drumstick, being careful not to tear the skin. Using your hand, spread a generous amount of the rosemary mixture under the breast skin and down the thigh and leg. Rub the remainder of the rosemary mixture over the outside of the breast. Use toothpicks to seal skin over any exposed breast meat. Place the turkey on a rack in a roasting pan. Add about ¼" of water to the bottom of the pan. Roast in the preheated oven 3 to 4 hours, or until the internal temperature of the bird reaches 180 degrees F (80 degrees C). #Delish!

Savory Guatemalan Roast Turkey

½ cup raw pumpkin seeds
1 (10 pound) whole turkey, neck and giblets removed
1 (5 ounce) jar pitted green olives, drained
1 Granny Smith apple, peeled, quartered, and cored
1 large green bell pepper, halved and seeded
1 onion, cut into chunks
10 large Roma (plum) tomatoes, halved and seeded
2 bay leaves
2 dried ancho chills, stemmed and seeded
2 tablespoons vegetable oil
Salt and pepper to taste

Place an oven rack in the topmost position and preheat oven on the broil setting. Line a baking sheet with aluminum foil. Place tomatoes and bell pepper onto the baking sheet, cut-side down. Broil on top rack of preheated oven until the skins begin to blacken, about 5 minutes. Place charred vegetables into a bowl and seal with plastic wrap to steam until their skins begin to give. Lower the oven rack to make room, and turn heat oven to 325 degrees. Meanwhile, pour vegetable oil into a roasting pan (or skillet that can accommodate the size of the turkey), and place over medium-high heat. When hot, add the turkey and sear on all sides until browned, about 10 minutes. Once the turkey has been browned, place breast side up into the roasting pan, and stuff with quartered apples and olives. Set aside. Next, heat a skillet over medium-high heat. Add the ancho chilies, pumpkin seeds and bay leaves. Cook and stir until the pumpkin seeds begin to smell toasted, about 5 minutes, and then pour the mixture into a blender. Once the tomatoes and peppers have steamed enough that the skins have loosened, remove and discard the skins. Place tomatoes, green peppers, and onion into the blender with the pumpkin seeds. Blend to a smooth and thick sauce. Season with salt and pepper to taste. Add olive juice for additional flavor if desired. Brush the sauce onto the turkey, and place into your preheated oven. Cook until a meat thermometer inserted in the thickest part of the thigh reaches 180 degrees F (85 degrees C), about 3 hours. Baste occasionally until done. #Delish!

Leftover & Select Turkey Cuts

Apple Turkey
½ pound turkey breast tenderloins
½ teaspoon chicken bouillon granules
1 medium tart apple, sliced
1 tablespoon butter or margarine
1 tablespoon cider vinegar
1 teaspoon Dijon mustard
2 tablespoons maple syrup
In a large skillet, cook turkey in butter over medium heat for 4-5 minutes on each side or until the juices run clear. Remove from the skillet; cover and keep warm. In the same skillet, combine the syrup, vinegar, mustard and bouillon. Add the apple; cook and stir over medium heat for 2-3 minutes or until apple is tender. Spoon over turkey. #Delish!

Awesome Turkey Spinach Casserole (low fat)
¼ cup chopped red onion
¼ cup fat-free Parmesan cheese topping
½ cup reduced-fat mayonnaise
½ cup water
½ teaspoon dried parsley flakes
½ teaspoon garlic powder
¾ cup uncooked instant brown rice
1 (10 oz.) package frozen chopped spinach, thawed and squeezed dry
1 (10.75 oz.) can reduced-fat condensed cream of chicken soup, undiluted
1 medium yellow squash, cubed
1 teaspoon ground mustard
1/8 teaspoon paprika
1/8 teaspoon pepper
2 cups cubed cooked turkey breast
In a large bowl, combine the soup, mayonnaise and water. Stir in everything except Parmesan and paprika. Transfer to a shallow 2.5 quart baking dish coated with nonstick cooking spray. Cover and bake at 350 degrees for 35-40 minutes or until rice is tender. Uncover; sprinkle with Parmesan topping and paprika. Bake an additional five minutes. #Delish!

Baked Turkey Mac N' Cheese
¼ teaspoon pepper
1 (10.75 ounce) can condensed cream of chicken soup, undiluted
1 (8 ounce) can mushroom stems and pieces, drained
1 ½ cups uncooked elbow macaroni
1 cup milk
2 cups cubed cooked turkey
2 cups shredded cheddar cheese, divided
In a large bowl, combine the turkey, macaroni, 1 ½ cups cheese, soup, milk, mushrooms and pepper. Pour into a greased 2 quarts baking dish. Cover and bake at 350 degrees for 60-65 minutes or until macaroni is tender. Uncover; sprinkle with remaining cheese. Bake 5-10 minutes longer or until cheese is melted. Serve hot. #Delish!

Celestial Citrus Turkey
¼ cup orange juice
¼ cup water
¼ cup white wine or additional chicken broth
½ teaspoon pepper
½ teaspoon salt
1 cup chicken broth, divided
1 tablespoon garlic powder
1 tablespoon lemon juice
1 tablespoon olive oil
1 tablespoon paprika
2 tablespoons cornstarch
2 teaspoons Worcestershire sauce
3 pounds frozen boneless turkey roast, thawed
8 cloves garlic, peeled
Cut roast in half. Combine the garlic powder, paprika, oil, Worcestershire sauce, salt and pepper; rub over turkey. Place in a 5-quart slow cooker. Add the garlic, ⅓ cup broth, water, wine or additional broth, orange juice and lemon juice. Cover and cook on low for 5-6 hours or until a meat thermometer reads 170 degrees. Remove turkey and keep warm. Discard garlic cloves. If gravy is desired, combine cornstarch and remaining broth until smooth. Stir into cooking juices. Cover and cook on high for 15 minutes or until thickened. Slice turkey; serve with gravy and favorite sides. #Delish!

Cheesy Tukey Omelets

¼ cup diced green pepper
½ cup shredded Monterey Jack cheese
½ teaspoon minced garlic
1/3 cup chopped onion
3 tablespoons butter, divided
3 tablespoons water
4 ounces smoked turkey
6 eggs

In a large skillet, cook the turkey, onion, green pepper and garlic in 2 tablespoons butter until vegetables are tender. Remove and keep warm. In the same skillet, melt remaining butter. In a bowl, beat the eggs and water. Pour into skillet; cook over medium heat. As eggs set, lift the edges, letting uncooked portion flow underneath. When eggs are nearly set, spoon turkey mixture over half of the omelet. Fold omelet over filling. Sprinkle with cheese. Cover and let stand for 1-2 minutes or until cheese is melted. Serve with a side of fresh fruit. #Delish!

Creamy Turkey Tortellini Alfredo

¼ cup milk
½ cup shredded mozzarella cheese
1 (15 ounce) jar prepared Alfredo sauce
1 (9 ounce) package refrigerated cheese tortellini
1 teaspoon minced garlic
2 cups cubed cooked turkey
2 tablespoons butter
2 tablespoons grated Parmesan cheese
Salt and pepper to taste

Bring a saucepan of lightly salted water to a boil, stir in the tortellini, reduce heat, and simmer until pasta is just tender, about 5 minutes. Drain the tortellini in a colander set in the sink. Preheat oven to 325 degrees. Grease a 1½- quart baking dish and set aside. Heat the butter in a skillet over medium heat. Cook and stir the garlic until fragrant, about 2 minutes. Whisk in the Alfredo sauce and milk; season to taste with salt and pepper. Bring the mixture to a simmer over medium-low heat. Stir in the tortellini and turkey, mixing enough to coat the pasta and turkey with the sauce. Spoon the mixture into the prepared baking dish, and sprinkle the top with mozzarella and Parmesan cheeses. Bake in the preheated oven until the casserole is bubbling and the cheese topping has melted and begun to brown, about 15 to 20 minutes. #Delish!

Curried Turkey
¼ cup milk
¼ cup onion, minced
½ teaspoon curry powder
1 (10.75 ounce) can condensed cream of mushroom soup
1 (6 ounce) can sliced mushrooms, drained
1 ½ cups uncooked rice
1 cup sour cream
1 tablespoon butter
2 cups cooked turkey meat, chopped or shredded
3 cups water
In a saucepan, bring water to a boil. Add rice and stir. Reduce heat, cover and simmer for 20 minutes. In a medium saucepan over medium heat, melt the butter, Sauté the onion until translucent, not browned. Reduce the heat to a simmer, and stir in the mushroom soup, drained mushrooms, and milk. Heat while stirring constantly until the mixture is smooth. Add the sour cream, curry powder, and turkey meat, stirring continuously. Cover and allow to low simmer 20 to 25 minutes. Ladle the curry mixture evenly over the rice for each individual serving. #Delish!

Day After Turkey Day Salad
½ cup finely chopped pepperoncini
½ cup mayonnaise (not Miracle Whip)
¾ cup shredded cheddar cheese
1/8 teaspoon crushed red pepper
2 cups leftover turkey, coarsely chopped
2 tablespoons cooked bacon, crumbled
2 tablespoons dill pickle relish
3 tablespoons prepared yellow mustard
Salt to taste
Stir together mayonnaise, mustard, bacon, cheese, relish, pepperoncini, red pepper, and salt in a large bowl; add the turkey and stir to coat. Mix well and serve. #Delish!

Delish Broccoli Salad
¼ cup olive or vegetable oil
½ cup thinly sliced red onion
1 (8 oz.) can unsweetened pineapple chunks
1 green bell pepper, julienned
1 tablespoon poppy seeds
2 cups broccoli florets
2 cups cubed cooked turkey
2 cups torn fresh spinach
2 cups torn salad greens
2 tablespoons red wine or balsamic vinegar
2 teaspoons Dijon mustard
2 teaspoons sugar
Drain the pineapple, reserving 2 tablespoons juice; set aside. In a large bowl, combine the greens, spinach, broccoli, green pepper, onion, turkey

and pineapple. In a small bowl, combine oil, vinegar, poppy seeds, sugar, mustard and reserved pineapple juice; mix well. Pour over salad and toss to coat. Serve immediately. #Delish!

Drunken Turkey Dish

¼ cup half-and-half cream
½ teaspoon ground black pepper
½ teaspoon onion powder
½ teaspoon salt
1 (10.75 ounce) can condensed cream of chicken soup
1 (10.75 ounce) can water
1 teaspoon vegetable oil
1 (8 ounce) package sliced fresh mushrooms
1 bay leaf
1 cup shredded cooked turkey breast
1 small carrot, diced
1 tablespoon butter
1 teaspoon dried parsley flakes
1/3 cup dry sherry
2/3 cup frozen peas

Stir the cream of chicken soup into the one soup can of water in a bowl. Heat vegetable oil in a large saucepan over medium heat, stir in mushrooms and carrot, and cook and stir until mushrooms and carrot begins to soften, about 5 minutes. Add shredded turkey, onion powder, salt, pepper, bay leaf, and sherry to the pan and cook, stirring another 5 minutes to reduce pan juices and cook off the alcohol from the wine. Pour the soup over the turkey mixture and bring to a boil. Reduce heat and add the half-and-half, parsley, and frozen peas. Simmer 5 to 10 minutes to reduce the sauce and heat the peas through. Remove bay leaf and stir in butter just before serving. #Delish!

Easy Italian Turkey Salad

¼ cup red onions, sliced
½ cup carrots, sliced
½ cup celery, sliced
½ cup green pepper, sliced
½ cup red pepper, sliced
1/3 cup vinegar
2 cups favorite pasta, cooked
2/3 cup oil
8 oz. leftover turkey, diced

In a large bowl, combine turkey, vinegar, oil, and vegetables. Toss to coat. Cover and refrigerate until serving time. Spoon turkey mixture over cooked pasta. Mix well and serve. #Delish!

Easy Turkey Dumpling Soup
½ cup chopped carrot
½ cup chopped celery
½ cup chopped onion
½ teaspoon dill weed
½ teaspoon pepper
½ teaspoon poultry seasoning
1 cup frozen peas
1 egg
1 leftover turkey carcass
2 ½ cups all-purpose flour
2 bay leaves
2 teaspoons salt
3 tablespoons dried parsley flakes
5 quarts water
Place the first nine ingredients in a Dutch oven or soup kettle. Bring to a boil; skim fat. Reduce heat; cover and simmer for 2 hours. Remove bay leaves. Remove carcass; allow to cool. Remove turkey from bones and cut into bite-size pieces; set aside. Pour 1 cup of the broth into a bowl; add egg and beat. Stir in enough flour to form a stiff dough. Turn onto a floured surface; knead 8-10 times or until smooth. Next, divide dough in half and roll out each piece to 1/8" thickness. Cut into 2" x ¼" strips. Add dill and poultry seasoning to remaining broth; bring to a gentle boil. Drop dough strips into broth; cover and cook for 30-35 minutes or until tender. Add peas and reserved turkey; heat through and serve. #Delish!

Fun Florentine Turkey Breast
¼ teaspoon pepper
½ teaspoon salt
¾ cup chopped onion
¾ teaspoon dried tarragon
1 (10 ounce) package frozen chopped spinach, thawed and squeezed dry
1 (3 pound) turkey breast half, bone removed
1 (4.5 ounce) jar sliced mushrooms, drained
1 ½ cups milk
1 tablespoon butter, melted
1/3 cup cubed process cheese (Velveeta type)
3 tablespoons all-purpose flour
5 bacon strips
Cut a lengthwise slit in turkey breast to within ½" of opposite side; open meat so it lies flat. Cover with plastic wrap and flatten with mallet to ½" thickness. Remove plastic wrap; set aside. In a skillet, cook two bacon strips until crisp. Drain, reserving 2 tablespoons drippings. Crumble bacon and set aside. Next, in the drippings, sauté onion until tender. Stir in flour, tarragon, salt and pepper until blended. Gradually stir in milk. Bring to a boil; cook and stir for 2 minutes or until thickened. Remove from heat. Refrigerate ½ cup sauce. Add the spinach, mushrooms and crumbled bacon to the remaining sauce; spread over turkey breast. Starting at a short end, roll up and tuck in ends; tie with kitchen string. Place on a rack in a greased roasting pan. Brush with butter. Cover loosely with foil. Bake

at 350 degrees for 1 hour. Remove foil. Cut remaining bacon strips in half; place over the turkey. Bake 25-35 minutes longer. Discard string. Let turkey stand for 10 minutes before slicing. Meanwhile, heat the reserved sauce; stir in cheese until melted. Serve with the turkey. #Delish!

Glorious Grape Turkey Salad
1 (8 ounce) package mostaccioli pasta
1 ½ cups mayonnaise
1 cup chopped celery
1 cup sour cream
1 head romaine lettuce leaves, torn into bite size pieces
1 tablespoon minced celery root
2 cups diced cooked turkey
2 cups halved seedless red grapes

Bring a large pot of lightly salted water to a boil. Add pasta and cook until just tender. Drain and run under cold water to cool. Transfer to a large bowl. Set aside. In a separate bowl, stir together the mayonnaise, sour cream and celery root. Stir this into the noodles to coat. Next, fold in the grapes, turkey and celery. Chill until serving. #Delish!

Gobbler Pita Tacos
¼ teaspoon pepper
¼ teaspoon salt
1 (2.25 ounce) can sliced ripe olives, drained
1 cup cubed cooked turkey
1 cup shredded cheddar cheese
1 garlic clove, minced
1 medium green pepper, chopped
1 medium sweet red pepper, chopped
1 small tomato, chopped
1 cup chunky salsa
1 tablespoon cider or red wine vinegar
1 tablespoon vegetable oil
1 teaspoon chili powder
1 teaspoon ground cumin
3 green onions, thinly sliced
5 (6 inch) pita flat breads

In a small bowl, combine the first six ingredients; set aside. In a large bowl, combine the turkey, peppers, tomato, salsa, onions, olives and garlic. Stir the oil mixture; pour over the turkey mixture and mix well. Stir in cheese. On a lightly greased griddle, heat pita breads on both sides. Spoon about ½ cup turkey mixture into each half. Fold over and enjoy!

Green Bean Turkey Surprise
½ cup crushed cheese flavored crackers
1 (10.75 ounce) can condensed cream of mushroom soup, undiluted
1 ½ cups cubed cooked turkey breast
1 cup shredded cheddar cheese
1/3 cup milk
2 cups frozen cut green beans, thawed
3 cups mashed potatoes
In a 2-quart microwave-safe dish, combine the green beans, turkey, soup, cheese and milk. Cover and microwave on high for 5-6 minutes or until bubbly, stirring once. Carefully spread mashed potatoes over turkey mixture; sprinkle with cracker crumbs. Cover and cook on high for 2-4 minutes or until heated through. Let stand for 5 minutes before serving. #Delish!

Happy Holiday Medley
½ (15 ounce) can peas, drained
½ cup all-purpose flour
½ small onion
1 (4 ounce) jar pimentos (optional)
1 (4.5 ounce) can mushrooms, drained
1 green bell pepper, chopped
2 cups milk
2/3 cup butter
3 celery, chopped
4 cups cooked turkey, chopped
In a large saucepan over medium heat, melt butter. Slowly cook and stir onion and celery until soft. Mix flour into saucepan and stir until vegetables are evenly coated. Stir in milk and allow the mixture to thicken. Mix in the turkey, mushrooms, pimentos, bell pepper and peas. Stir and cook until thick; thin with milk if desired. #Delish

Hot Pepper Turkey Spread
¼ teaspoon hot pepper sauce
¼ teaspoon pepper
½ cup chicken broth
1 ½ cups ketchup
1 ½ teaspoons Worcestershire sauce
1 small green pepper, chopped
1 small onion, chopped
1 teaspoon prepared mustard
2 tablespoons butter or margarine
3 cups cubed cooked turkey
Hot cooked rice
In a large saucepan, melt butter; sauté onion and green pepper until tender. Stir in ketchup, broth, Worcestershire sauce, mustard, hot pepper sauce and pepper. Add turkey. Simmer, uncovered, for 20 minutes or until heated through. Serve over rice or on rolls for sandwiches. #Delish!

Hot Turkey Parmesan
¼ cup milk
¼ teaspoon black pepper
¾ cup sour cream
1 (10.75 ounce) can condensed cream of mushroom soup
1/3 cup grated parmesan cheese
2 cups chopped cooked turkey
3 cups frozen broccoli florets, thawed
8 ounces spaghetti, broken in half, uncooked
Preheat oven to 350 degrees. Cook spaghetti as directed on package; drain. Mix soup, sour cream, milk, Parmesan cheese and pepper in large bowl. Add spaghetti, broccoli and turkey; mix lightly. Spoon into 2- quart casserole. Bake 25 to 30 minutes or until heated through.

Hot Turkey Salad
½ cup cheddar cheese, grated
½ cup pecans, chopped
½ teaspoon salt
1 cup mayonnaise
1 cup potato chips, crushed
2 cups celery, chopped
2 cups cubed cooked turkey
2 tablespoons fresh lemon juice
2 teaspoons grated onion
Preheat oven to 450 degrees. Grease a 9x13" baking dish. Mix the turkey, celery, onion, pecans, and salt together in a mixing bowl. Stir in the mayonnaise and lemon juice until evenly blended. Spoon into the prepared baking dish. Sprinkle with cheddar cheese, then potato chips. Bake in preheated oven until cheese melts, 10 to 12 minutes. #Delish!

Island Dream Turkey Salad
¼ teaspoon curry powder
½ cup chopped green onion
1 cup chopped orange segments
1 cup diced celery
1 cup diced red bell pepper
1 cup pineapple chunks
1 tablespoon fresh lemon juice
1 tablespoon honey
1/3 cup low-fat sour cream
2 tablespoons apricot preserves or jam
4 cups chopped cooked turkey
Blend sour cream, apricot jam, lemon juice, honey, and curry powder in a small bowl. Mix well and refrigerate until ready to use. In a large bowl, combine turkey, red pepper, celery, pineapple, orange segments, and green onion. Add refrigerated dressing and toss well to coat. Refrigerate for 1 hour before serving. #Delish!

Italian Turkey Pasta

½ (16 ounce) package whole wheat spaghetti
1 (26 ounce) jar spaghetti sauce
1 cup shredded mozzarella cheese
1 green bell pepper, chopped
1 pound cubed cooked turkey
1 small red onion, thinly sliced
Olive oil

Fill a large pot with lightly salted water and bring to a rolling boil. Stir in the spaghetti, and return to a boil. Cook uncovered, stirring occasionally, until the pasta has cooked, but is still a bit firm, about 12 minutes. Drain well in a colander and set aside. Meanwhile, heat the olive oil in a large saucepan or Dutch oven over medium heat. Stir in the onion and green pepper. Cook and stir until the onion has softened and turned translucent, about 5 minutes. Stir in the turkey and spaghetti sauce. Bring to a simmer over medium- high heat, then cover, and reduce heat to medium-low. Cook until the sauce is hot. Once the spaghetti has been cooked and drained, stir it into the hot sauce along with the mozzarella cheese. Stir until the cheese melts, then serve. #Delish!

Jamaican Turkey Sandwiches & Coleslaw

¼ cup sweet chili sauce
½ cup chopped celery
½ cup juice from canned pineapple
1 (2 pound) skinless, boneless turkey breast, cut into 8 ounce chunks
1 tablespoon beef bouillon granules
1/3 cup chopped green onion
2 tablespoons water
2 teaspoons garlic powder
3 tablespoons distilled white vinegar
6 canned pineapple rings
6 Kaiser rolls, split

COLESLAW TOPPING:
¼ cup mayonnaise
½ cup chopped onion
1 cup shredded cheddar cheese
1 tablespoon lemon juice
2 cups chopped cabbage
2 tablespoons chopped fresh parsley
Salt and black pepper to taste

Sprinkle the celery and green onions into the bottom of a slow cooker; place the turkey chunks on top. Combine the pineapple juice, sweet chili sauce, vinegar, water, beef bouillon, and garlic powder; pour over the turkey. Place the pineapple rings on the turkey chunks. Cook on the low setting until the turkey pulls apart easily, 6 to 7 hours. Meanwhile, make the coleslaw by stirring the mayonnaise, lemon juice, parsley, and onion together in a mixing bowl. Add the cabbage and cheese; season to taste with salt and pepper. Cover, and refrigerate while the turkey cooks. Once the turkey is tender, shred using two forks. Pile some of the shredded turkey and a pineapple ring onto a Kaiser roll; top with coleslaw to serve. #Delish!

Lemon Turkey with Couscous Stuffing
¼ teaspoon salt
½ teaspoon grated lemon peel
1 (4 pound) bone-in turkey breast
1 garlic clove, minced
1 teaspoon lemon juice
1/8 teaspoon pepper
2 teaspoons olive oil
STUFFING:
¼ cup slivered almonds, toasted
½ cup raisins
1 ½ cups boiling water
1 cup uncooked couscous
1 medium carrot, shredded
1/3 cup chicken broth
2 tablespoons minced fresh parsley

Carefully loosen turkey skin, leaving it attached at the back. Combine the oil, lemon juice, garlic, lemon peel, salt and pepper; spread under turkey skin. Place turkey to one side in a shallow roasting pan coated with nonstick cooking spray. *For stuffing*: In a bowl, pour boiling water over couscous. Cover and let stand for 5 minutes or until water is absorbed. Add the remaining ingredients; toss to combine. Spoon stuffing into other side of pan, shaping into a nice size mound. Cover pan and bake at 325 degrees for 45 minutes. Then uncover turkey, but leave stuffing covered. Bake 40-50 minutes longer or until a meat thermometer reads 170 degrees. Cover turkey with foil and let stand for 15 minutes before slicing. Serve with stuffing. #Delish!

Lemony Turkey Soup
¼ cup lemon juice
¼ cup minced fresh cilantro or parsley
¼ teaspoon pepper
1 (10.75 ounce) can condensed cream of chicken soup, undiluted
2 cups cooked rice
2 cups diced cooked turkey
2 tablespoons cornstarch
6 cups chicken broth, divided

In a large saucepan, combine 5 ½ cups of broth, soup, rice, turkey and pepper. Bring to a boil; boil for 3 minutes. In a small bowl, combine cornstarch and remaining broth until smooth. Gradually stir into hot soup. Cook and stir for 1-2 minutes or until thickened and heated through. Remove from the heat; stir in lemon juice and cilantro. #Delish!

Melon Medley Turkey Salad

¼ cup reduced-fat mayonnaise
½ cup chopped unsalted dry roasted cashews
½ cup fat-free plain yogurt
½ teaspoon ground ginger
1 ½ cups seedless red grapes, halved
1 cup chopped celery
1 teaspoon lemon juice
1/8 teaspoon salt
4 cups cubed cooked turkey breast
4 medium cantaloupes, halved and seeded

Make melon balls from one cantaloupe half; refrigerate remaining cantaloupe halves. In a large bowl, combine the turkey, grapes, celery and cantaloupe balls. In a small bowl, combine the yogurt, mayonnaise, lemon juice, ginger and salt. Pour over turkey mixture and stir gently to coat. Cover and refrigerate for 1 hour. Stir in cashews just before serving. Spoon 1 cup salad into each cantaloupe half. #Delish!

Mucho Turkey Burrito

¼ cup self-rising flour
1 (8 ounce) package shredded cheddar cheese
1 cup leftover gravy
1 cup mashed potatoes
1 cup prepared stuffing
1 large onion, chopped
1 tablespoon dried parsley
10 (10 inch) flour tortillas
2 quarts turkey broth
3 cups cooked turkey, cut into bite-size pieces
3 pickled jalapeno peppers, sliced
3 tablespoons pickled jalapeno pepper juice
Salt and pepper to taste

In a large pot, combine turkey, stuffing, mashed potatoes, gravy, broth, and onion. Bring to a boil, and cook until onion is soft. Thicken with flour if needed. Warm tortillas in a dry frying pan over medium heat. Spoon turkey mixture onto a warm tortilla, sprinkle with cheese, and roll into a burrito. Repeat with remaining ingredients. Spread more cheese on top and add another spoonful of the turkey mixture over the cheese. Garnish with jalapeno slices, sprinkle with jalapeno juice, and season with salt, pepper, and parsley. Serve hot. #Delish!

Navaho Turkey Soup
½ teaspoon cayenne pepper
½ teaspoon dried cilantro
½ teaspoon ground cumin
1 (28 ounce) can whole peeled tomatoes
1 (4 ounce) can chopped green chili peppers
1 ½ cups cooked turkey, shredded
1 avocado - peeled, pitted and diced
1 cup shredded Monterey Jack cheese
1 onion, chopped
1 tablespoon lime juice
2 cloves garlic, crushed
2 Roma (plum) tomatoes, chopped
4 cups vegetable broth
Salt and pepper to taste
In a large pot over medium heat, combine turkey, broth, canned tomatoes, green chilies, fresh tomatoes, onion, garlic, and lime juice. Season with cayenne, cumin, salt, and pepper. Bring to a boil, then reduce heat, and simmer 15 to 20 minutes. Stir in avocado and cilantro, and simmer 15 to 20 minutes, until slightly thickened. Spoon into serving bowls, and top with shredded cheese. #Delish!

New Year's Turkey Salad
¼ teaspoon salt
½ cup coarsely chopped walnuts
½ cup dried cranberries
½ cup sour cream
1 cup diced celery
1 cup mayonnaise
1 tablespoon chopped fresh rosemary
1/8 teaspoon black pepper
2 tablespoons chopped fresh parsley
3 cups diced cooked turkey
Mix the turkey, celery, cranberries, and walnuts together in a bowl. To prepare the salad dressing, whisk the mayonnaise, sour cream, parsley, rosemary, salt, and pepper together in a bowl. Pour over the turkey mixture, and toss to coat evenly. Refrigerate the salad for at least 1 hour. Serve cold. #Delish!

Pumpkin Turkey Chili

1 (14.5 oz.) can diced tomatoes
1 ½ tablespoon chili powder
1 bell pepper, chopped (your choice of color!)
1 large can tomato sauce
1 large onion, chopped
1 lb. leftover chopped turkey, diced fine
1 tablespoon olive oil
1 teaspoon cumin
1 teaspoon paprika
2 (14.5 oz.) can of your favorite beans (kidney, black, garbanzo!)
2 carrots, chopped
2 cups pumpkin puree
2 stalks celery, chopped
2-3 garlic cloves, minced (to taste0
Salt and ground pepper, taste
Shredded cheddar cheese
Sour cream

In a large pot, heat the olive oil and sauté the onions, carrots, celery, peppers and garlic until tender. Add the ground turkey and cook until evenly browned. Pour into a slow cooker or keep in the large Dutch oven or pot. Mix in tomatoes, sauce, pumpkin and any spices of your choice. Cook over very low heat or in slow cooker for 4-5 hours, adding water as needed. Stir hourly. Serve with a spoonful of sour cream and shredded cheddar cheese on top. #Delish!

Roasted Turkey Walkers

¼ cup balsamic vinegar
¼ cup molasses
½ cup brown sugar
½ cup ketchup
½ cup pomegranate molasses
½ cup salt
½ cup white sugar
2 cups white wine
2 tablespoons Worcestershire sauce
4 tablespoons dried sage leaves, divided
4 tablespoons dried thyme leaves, divided
4 turkey drumsticks

Place the salt and sugar into a large resealable bag. Pour in enough water to cover the turkey legs, and squeeze the bag to dissolve and mix salt and sugar. Immerse turkey legs in the brine, and seal the bag. Refrigerate for at least 2 hours. Next, in a saucepan, stir together the white wine, both molasses, brown sugar, vinegar, ketchup and Worcestershire sauce. Bring to a boil, and cook until reduced by half. Season with 1 tablespoon of sage and 1 tablespoon of thyme. Taste and adjust sugar, salt and pepper if desired. To cook turkey, preheat the oven to 325 degrees. Remove the turkey legs from the brine and pat dry with paper towels. Heat a large skillet (preferably cast-iron) over medium-high heat. Fry the turkey, turning frequently, until browned on all sides. Place the pan with the turkey into the oven. Roast uncovered for 45 minutes in the preheated oven. Remove and turn legs over. Season with some of the remaining thyme and sage, and spoon some of the sauce onto the legs to coat. Return to the oven for an additional 30 minutes. Repeat the seasoning and baste with the sauce again, and return to the oven. Roast for 15 more minutes, then test. The internal temperature taken at the thickest part of the thigh should be 180 degrees when taken with a meat thermometer. Serve turkey with remaining sauce on the side. #Delish!

Simple Turkey Mex
½ cup water
1 large fresh tomato, chopped
1 onion, chopped
1 pound shredded cooked turkey
1 tablespoon chopped fresh cilantro
1 teaspoon garlic powder
1 teaspoon vegetable oil
Salt and pepper to taste
Heat the oil in a skillet over medium heat, and cook the onion until tender. Mix in turkey, and season with garlic powder. Stir in the tomato. Pour in water, sprinkle with cilantro, and season with salt and pepper. Cover skillet, and simmer 5 minutes, or until heated through. #Delish!

Slow Cooker Turkey Stew
¼ cup dried onion flakes
¼ cup white wine
¼ teaspoon dried thyme leaves
¼ teaspoon garlic powder
½ teaspoon dried Italian seasoning
½ teaspoon lemon pepper seasoning
1 (28 ounce) can canned stewed tomatoes
3 lbs. turkey meat, cubed (preferably thigh meat)
6 cubes chicken bouillon
Pour tomatoes and wine into slow cooker. Stir in bouillon cubes, onion flakes, lemon pepper, Italian seasoning, garlic powder, and thyme; stir. Add turkey. Cover and cook on lowest setting for 8 to 10 hours until the turkey meat pulls apart easily. #Delish!

Spicy Turkey Wraps with Strawberry Salsa

¼ cup finely chopped cilantro
½ cup finely chopped red onion
1 (1 ounce) package Southwest marinade seasoning
1 cup crumbled blue cheese
1 jalapeno pepper, seeded and minced
1 pound strawberries, diced
1 tablespoon fresh lime juice
1 tablespoon vegetable oil
1 teaspoon sea salt
2 cups fresh baby spinach
2 pounds turkey tenderloins, cut into ½" slices
4 (10 inch) flavored tortillas
Fresh ground pepper

In a medium bowl, toss the turkey with the Southwest marinade seasoning to coat, and allow to stand for 15 minutes. Meanwhile, prepare a strawberry salsa by stirring together the diced strawberries, red onion, cilantro, jalapeno pepper, and lime juice in a bowl. Season to taste with salt and pepper; set aside. Heat vegetable oil in a large skillet over medium-high heat. Add turkey, and cook until firm and lightly browned, about 5 minutes. Once done, microwave the tortillas for 30 seconds. *To assemble*: Evenly divide the cooked turkey onto each tortilla. Top with spinach, blue cheese and strawberry salsa, and roll into a wrap. Garnish with jalapenos if desired. #Delish!!

Stuffed Teriyaki Turkey Legs

1 cup olive oil
1 large white onion
1 pinch ground black pepper
1 teaspoon dried oregano
2 green bell peppers
2 tablespoons distilled white vinegar
2 tablespoons salt
2 tablespoons bottled teriyaki sauce
4 turkey legs
5 slices bacon

Make numerous vertical slits in the turkey legs. In a small bowl combine the olive oil with the salt, pepper, teriyaki, vinegar and oregano. Marinate turkey legs in oil mixture. Cut onion, green pepper and bacon into small squares (approximately the same size as the slits you cut on the legs). Fill each slit with one piece of pepper, onion and bacon. After the legs are stuffed, brown them in the oil in a skillet with deep sides over medium-high heat. Reduce heat to low and cover. Cook for 45 minutes or until meat starts to separate from the bone. Add water if turkey starts to dry out. #Delish!

Sunny Turkey Salad
¼ cups mayonnaise
¼ cups raisins
¼ cups roasted sunflower seeds
¼ teaspoon salt
2 cups leftover turkey (cooked)
2 small apples, diced
Juice of ¼ lemon
Mix all ingredients in a salad bowl. Refrigerate for a minimum of 2 hours. Serve chilled. #Delish!

Terrific Turkey Enchiladas
1 (19 ounce) can red enchilada sauce
1 (2 ounce) can sliced black olives
1 onion, chopped
2 cups shredded cheddar and Monterey cheese blend
24 (6 inch) corn tortillas
4 cups cooked turkey, chopped
Preheat oven to 350 degrees. Lightly grease a 9x13" baking dish. In a small bowl, combine the cheese, onion, and black olives. In a small skillet, heat enough oil to lightly coat one tortilla, and cook until soft. Remove and dip in enchilada sauce to coat. Add turkey and cheese mixture to center of tortilla, roll and place in the prepared dish. Repeat until bottom layer of pan is covered with enchiladas. Spread enough sauce over bottom layer to cover. Repeat the entire process with a second layer. Spread all remaining sauce on top and sprinkle with remaining cheese mixture. Bake 20 minutes in the preheated oven, or until cheese is melted. #Delish!

Top-Notch Turkey Casserole
¼ cup grated carrot
¼ cup sliced celery
¼ cup uncooked wild rice
¼ cup white wine or chicken broth
½ cup fresh broccoli florets
½ teaspoon dried marjoram
½ teaspoon dried oregano
1 (2 ounce) jar diced pimientos, drained
1 ¾ cups uncooked long grain rice
1 small onion, chopped
1 teaspoon salt
2 cups shredded cheddar cheese, divided
2 cups shredded Swiss cheese
2 cups sliced fresh mushrooms
2 tablespoons olive or vegetable oil
3 cups milk
4 cups chicken broth
5 cups cubed cooked turkey
5 tablespoons all-purpose flour
In a large saucepan, bring broth to a boil; add the wild rice. Cover and simmer for 25 minutes. Add the long grain rice; simmer 25 minutes longer

or until tender. In a large skillet, sauté the mushrooms, broccoli, onion, carrot and celery in oil until tender. Add the turkey, pimientos, salt, marjoram and oregano. Stir in the rice. In a large saucepan, combine the flour, milk and wine or broth until smooth. bring to a boil; cook and stir for 2 minutes or until thickened. Stir in the Swiss cheese and 1 cup cheddar cheese until melted. Add to turkey mixture. Transfer to a greased baking dish. Sprinkle with the remaining cheddar cheese. Bake, uncovered, at 350 degrees for 25-30 minutes or until heated through. #Delish!

Turkey Deluxe
¼ pimento, diced
½ cup butter
½ teaspoon onion salt
1 cup light cream
2 (7 oz.) bottles 7-Up or other lemon-lime soda
2 green peppers, cut into thin strips
2 tablespoons Worcestershire sauce
6 cups diced cooked turkey
6 tablespoons flour
Salt to taste
Cook green peppers in butter over low heat until softened. Blend in flour thoroughly then add pimento, Worcestershire sauce, onion salt, and salt. Stir in 7-Up and cream and continue to cook over low heat, stirring constantly until mixture thickens. Add turkey and continue to cook until thoroughly heated, stirring constantly. Serve over rice or noodles, if desired. #Delish!

Sumptuous Turkey & Mushrooms
¼ cup butter or margarine
¼ teaspoon pepper
½ cup frozen peas, defrosted
½ cup milk
½ teaspoon salt
1 (4 ounce) jar sliced pimentos, drained
1 cup chicken broth
1 cup diced green pepper
1 cup sliced fresh mushrooms
1/3 cup all-purpose flour
1/8 teaspoon curry powder
1/8 teaspoon dried tarragon
1/8 teaspoon ground coriander
2 cups diced, cooked turkey
6 shells puff pastry, baked
In a medium saucepan, melt butter over medium heat. Sauté green pepper and mushrooms until pepper are crisp-tender. Meanwhile, mix together flour and seasonings; stir into vegetables. Cook and stir until flour is moistened. Stir in broth and milk. Cook, stirring constantly, until thickened. Add turkey and peas; heat through. Gently stir in pimientos. Spoon into shells and serve immediately. #Delish!

Turkey & Stuffing Pie
½ cup chopped onion
½ teaspoon dried thyme
1 (12 ounce) jar turkey gravy
1 (4 ounce) can mushroom stems and pieces, drained
1 cup chicken broth
1 cup frozen peas
1 egg, beaten
1 tablespoon all-purpose flour
1 tablespoon butter or margarine
1 tablespoon minced fresh parsley
1 teaspoon Worcestershire sauce
1/3 cup butter or margarine, melted
3 cups cubed cooked turkey
5 cups herb-seasoned stuffing (use box mix if desired)
5 slices processed American cheese, cut into strips
In a large bowl, combine the egg, broth and butter. Add stuffing; mix well. Press into the bottom and sides of a greased 9" pie plate; set aside. In a skillet, sauté mushrooms and onion in butter until tender. Sprinkle with flour; mix well. Add turkey, peas, parsley, Worcestershire sauce and thyme; mix well. Stir in gravy. Bring to a boil; boil and stir for 2 minutes. Spoon into the crust. Bake at 375 degrees for 20 minutes. Arrange cheese strips in a lattice pattern over filling. Bake 5-10 minutes longer or until the cheese is melted. #Delish!

Turkey Citrus Salad
½ cup raspberry vinaigrette salad dressing
½ cup walnut halves
1 (15 ounce) can mandarin oranges, drained
2 cups leftover roast turkey, pulled into bite-sized pieces
2 cups sliced mushrooms
4 cups baby spinach leaves
4 cups mixed salad greens
8 ounces sugar snap peas, trimmed and halved
Toss snap peas, turkey meat, spinach leaves, mixed salad greens, mushrooms, mandarin orange pieces, walnuts, and raspberry vinaigrette dressing lightly in a salad bowl to combine, and serve. #Delish!

Turkey Noodle Soup
¼ cup red lentils
½ teaspoon dried dill
1 ½ tablespoons chicken bouillon granules
1 bay leaf
1 cup uncooked medium egg noodles
1/8 teaspoon celery seed
1/8 teaspoon garlic powder
2 tablespoons dried minced onion
2 cups cooked turkey meat
In a large bowl, mix lentils, minced onion, bouillon, dill, celery seed, garlic powder, bay leaf and noodles. Bring 8 cups water to boil in a large

saucepan over high heat. Stir in soup mix. Cover, reduce heat and simmer 15 minutes. Remove and discard bay leaf. Stir in 1 (10 ounce) package frozen mixed vegetables and 2 cups cooked and diced turkey meat. Cook 5 minutes or until vegetables and turkey are heated through and tender. Enjoy!

Turkey Pasta Divine

¼ cup shredded Swiss cheese
¼ teaspoon pepper
½ cup sliced fresh mushrooms
½ teaspoon chicken bouillon granules
¾ cup milk
1 cup diced, cooked turkey
1 tablespoon butter or margarine
1 tablespoon all-purpose flour
1/8 teaspoon salt
10 fresh asparagus spears, cut into 1" pieces
3 tablespoons shredded Parmesan cheese
4 ounces uncooked angel hair pasta

Cook pasta per package directions. In a saucepan, melt butter. Stir in the flour, bouillon, pepper and salt until smooth; gradually add milk. Bring to a boil; cook and stir 2 minutes or until thickened. Reduce heat; add cheeses and stir until smooth. Stir in the turkey, asparagus and mushrooms. Cook until heated through. Drain pasta and place in a serving bowl. Pour sauce mixture over pasta; toss gently to coat. #Delish!

Turkey Soup with Dressing Dumplings

1 (16 ounce) can jellied cranberry sauce
1 (16 ounce) can whole berry cranberry sauce
1 cup corn kernels
1 cup cubed turnips
1 cup fresh green beans, trimmed
1 cup peas
1 roast turkey carcass
1 tablespoon poultry seasoning
4 medium onions
5 stalks celery
6 cups leftover stuffing
6 egg whites
6 medium carrots
6 quarts water
Nonstick cooking spray
Salt and pepper to taste

Set the oven rack about 6" from the heat source and preheat the oven's broiler. Remove all meat from cooked turkey carcass and set aside. Arrange bones in a roasting pan and broil until browned on both sides. Transfer browned bones to large stock pot and cover with 6 quarts of water. Trim, peel, and chop the onions, carrots, and celery; add peels and ends of raw onions, celery, and carrots to the stock pot and reserve the cleaned vegetables for the soup. Simmer bones and vegetable scraps for 1 hour.

Turn off the heat and allow stock to cool for 20 minutes. Strain the stock, discarding the bones and vegetable scraps. Remove the fat from the stock by refrigerating the stock overnight and removing the hardened fat layer from the top or by skimming the fat from the top of the liquid with a ladle. Next, combine leftover stuffing and egg whites in a large bowl. Form the stuffing mixture into small balls and place on a microwave-safe plate. Microwave the dumplings on High for 1 ½ to 2 minutes. Heat a large skillet over medium heat, and coat with cooking spray. Add the dumplings and cook until they are golden brown on all sides. Remove from pan and set aside. Add the reserved and chopped turkey meat, onions, celery, and carrots to the strained soup stock; simmer for 1 hour. Stir in the peas, corn, green beans, and turnips; simmer until the vegetables are tender. Pour in the jellied and whole berry cranberry sauces, poultry seasoning, salt, and pepper; stir. When the cranberry sauce has dissolved into the soup add the cooked dumplings and heat through. #Delish!

Turkey Stuffed Peppers
½ cup chopped tomato
½ cup milk
½ pound ground turkey
½ teaspoon salt
1 garlic clove, minced
1 small onion, chopped
1 tablespoon all-purpose flour
1/8 teaspoon pepper
2 large green peppers, tops and seeds removed
2 tablespoons butter or margarine
4 tablespoons shredded cheddar cheese, divided

In a large saucepan, cook peppers in boiling water for 3 minutes. Drain and rinse with cold water; set aside. In a skillet, cook the turkey, onion and garlic over medium heat until meat is no longer pink; drain and set aside. In the same skillet, melt butter. Stir in flour, salt and pepper until smooth. Gradually add milk. Bring to a boil; cook and stir for 1-2 minutes or until thickened. Return turkey mixture to skillet. Stir in tomato and 2 tablespoons cheese; heat through. Spoon into peppers; sprinkle with the remaining cheese. Place in a greased 1 quart baking dish. Cover and bake at 350 degrees for 25-30 minutes or until peppers are tender. Filing should be hot. Serve and enjoy! #Delish!

Turkey Tetrazzini Delight

¼ teaspoon ground black pepper
½ cup butter
½ cup cooking sherry
1 (10 oz.) package frozen green peas
1 (16 oz.) package linguine pasta
1 cup grated Parmesan cheese
Paprika to taste
1 cup minced green bell pepper
1 cup minced onion
1 teaspoon salt
1 teaspoon Worcestershire sauce
2 (10.75 oz.) cans condensed cream of mushroom soup
2 (10.75 oz.) cans water
2 cups chicken broth
2 cups shredded sharp cheddar cheese
3 cups sliced fresh mushrooms
4 cups chopped cooked chicken breast

Bring a large pot of lightly salted water to a boil. Add pasta and cook for 8 to 10 minutes or until al dente; drain and set aside. Preheat oven to 375 degrees. Meanwhile, melt butter in a large saucepan over medium heat. Add mushrooms, onion and bell pepper and sauté until tender. Stir in cream of mushroom soup, chicken broth and water and cook, stirring, until heated through. Stir in pasta, Cheddar cheese, peas, sherry, Worcestershire sauce, salt, pepper and chicken. Mix well and transfer mixture to a lightly greased rectangular baking dish. Sprinkle with Parmesan cheese and paprika. Bake in the preheated oven for 25 to 35 minutes, or until heated through. Enjoy!

Turkey Wild Rice Soup
¼ cup chopped slivered almonds
¼ cup finely chopped celery
¼ cup finely chopped onion
½ teaspoon ground black pepper, or to taste
½ teaspoon kosher salt, or to taste
½ teaspoon lemon juice
¾ cup half-and-half cream
1/3 cup all-purpose flour
1/3 cup shredded carrot
2 cups chopped cooked turkey
2 cups water
2/3 cup uncooked wild rice
4 cups turkey broth
6 tablespoons butter
Bring the wild rice and water to a boil in a saucepan. Reduce heat to medium-low, cover, and simmer until the rice is tender but not mushy, 40 to 45 minutes. Drain off any excess liquid, fluff the rice with a fork, and cook uncovered for 5 minutes more. Set the cooked rice aside. Melt the butter in a soup pot over medium heat. Cook and stir the onion and celery until the onion is translucent, about 5 minutes. Stir in the flour, and cook until it turns a pale yellowish-brown color, 3 to 5 minutes. Gradually whisk in the turkey stock until no lumps of flour remain. Stir in the carrot. Bring the mixture to a simmer and cook, whisking constantly, until the stock is thick and smooth and the carrot is tender, about 2 more minutes. Stir in the wild rice, turkey, salt, pepper, and almonds. Return to a simmer, and cook 2 more minutes to heat the ingredients. Stir in the lemon juice and half-and-half; bring the soup almost to a boil, and serve hot. #Delish!

White Turkey Chili
½ cup dry white wine
½ cup low-sodium chicken broth
½ teaspoon coarsely ground black pepper
½ teaspoon ground ginger
½ teaspoon salt
1 ½ cups chopped onion
1 ½ cups shredded Monterey Jack cheese
1 ½ teaspoons ground cumin
1 bay leaf
1 tablespoon olive oil
2 cups shredded cooked turkey
2 cups white kidney beans (cannellini), undrained
2 fresh jalapeno peppers, chopped
2 tablespoons lime juice
2 teaspoons dried oregano
3 cloves garlic, minced
Heat the olive oil in a skillet over medium heat. Cook onion in oil until the onion has softened and turned translucent, about 5 minutes. Stir in garlic, oregano, cumin, and ginger; cook for another minute. Pour in chicken

broth and white wine, and then add the bay leaf. Cook uncovered until slightly reduced, about 5 to 8 minutes. Stir in turkey, beans, and jalapeno. Simmer uncovered for 10 minutes, stirring occasionally. Using back of spoon, mash ¼ of beans to thicken sauce. Reduce heat to low, and begin stirring in cheese ½ cup at a time. Stir until cheese is completely melted. Season with salt and pepper. Remove from heat and stir in lime juice. Serve hot. #Delish!

Zesty Turkey Cabbage Rolls

½ cup uncooked long grain white rice
½ teaspoon ground black pepper
½ teaspoon salt
2 (8 ounce) cans tomato sauce
2 cups water
1 egg, beaten
1 pound ground turkey
1 teaspoon Worcestershire sauce
1/3 cup chopped onion
16 large cabbage leaves
2 tablespoons olive oil
2 teaspoons lemon juice
2/3 (6 ounce) can tomato paste
3 tablespoons brown sugar
2 cups baby carrots, sliced lengthwise (optional)

In a pot, bring 1 cup water and rice to a boil. Reduce heat to low, cover and simmer for 20 minutes. Preheat oven to 350 degrees. Butter a 9x13" casserole dish. Bring a large pot of water to boil. Reduce heat to low and place cabbage leaves in pot. Simmer 4 to 5 minutes, until tender. Drain leaves and set aside. Heat oil in a skillet over medium heat and cook turkey and onion until turkey is brown and onion is tender. Next, transfer turkey and onion to a bowl, cool slightly, and mix in cooked rice, egg and 1 can tomato sauce. Season with salt and pepper. In a separate bowl, mix 1 can tomato sauce, tomato paste, remaining water, brown sugar, lemon juice and Worcestershire sauce. Scatter carrot slices evenly over bottom of casserole dish. Spread cabbage leaves on a flat surface and place about 2 tablespoons turkey mixture in the center of each leaf. Fold edges of leaves over filling, then roll into logs. Place cabbage rolls seam side down in dish over carrots. Pour sauce evenly over rolls. #Delish!

**Thank you for your purchase!
May you enjoy and be well!**

BONUS
Easy & Elegant Turkey Stuffing
½ cup unsalted butter
½ cup unsalted butter, melted
1 (16 ounce) package herb-seasoned dry bread stuffing mix
1 ½ cups orange liqueur
1 cup chopped pecans
1 cup raisins
1 large onion, chopped
1 pound spicy Italian sausage, casing removed
2 cups chicken broth
2 cups chopped celery
4 Granny Smith apples, peeled, cored and chopped
4 teaspoons chopped fresh sage
Salt and pepper to taste
Place the raisins in a small saucepan, and cover with 1 cup of liqueur. Bring to boil, remove from heat, and set aside. In a large skillet, melt ½ cup butter. Sauté the celery and onion in the butter for 10 minutes. Transfer to a large mixing bowl. In the same skillet, cook the sausage over medium to high heat until crumbled and evenly brown. Drain. Combine the sausage and stuffing mix with the celery and onion mixture. Stir in the raisins and liqueur, pecans, and apples. Mix in melted butter, chicken broth, ½ cup orange liqueur until the stuffing is fully moistened. Season with sage, salt, and pepper. #Delish!

World's Best Turkey Gravy
¼ cup all-purpose flour
¼ teaspoon celery salt
½ teaspoon ground black pepper
1 cup water
1 teaspoon poultry seasoning
1 teaspoon salt
5 cups turkey stock
In a medium saucepan, bring the turkey stock to a boil. In a small bowl, dissolve flour in water. Gradually whisk into the turkey stock. Season with poultry seasoning, salt, pepper, and celery salt. Bring to a boil, reduce heat, and simmer for 8 to 10 minutes, or until thickened. #Delish!

ABOUT THE AUTHOR

I am a Tennessee native and a connoisseur of great tastes. My culinary delights are inspired by my Southern roots.

I am from cornbread and cabbage, fried chicken and Kool-Aid soaked lemon slices.

I am from hen houses, persimmon trees and juicy, red tomatoes on the vine.

I am from sunflowers growing wild in summer and homemade ice cream in the winter.

I am from family reunions, blue collar men, happy housewives, and Sunday dinners.

I am from spiritual folks who didn't always get it right, but believed in the power of prayer – and taught it to their kids.

I am from the hottest of hot summers and kids running barefoot and free through thirsty Tennessee grass.

I am from a grandmother who sang gospel that was magic...song drenched air would tumble from her lungs, leap into your spirit and make you feel fantastic things.

I am from hard, heartfelt lessons about living and kitchens full of the perfume of love.

♥♥♥ *This book is from my heart to yours.* ♥♥♥

Find more cookbooks online at http://www.tinyurl.com/sodelishdish.

Made in United States
Orlando, FL
19 November 2024